Discover other cultures

Musical Instruments
Around The World

Meryl Doney

W
FRANKLIN WATTS
LONDON • SYDNEY

About this book

When you begin to study musical instruments from around the world you will be amazed at the number of ways that people have discovered to make music. They range from beating out a rhythm on a piece of wood to the astonishing *gamelan* orchestra of Java in Indonesia. All over the world, musicians have made use of local materials and methods to make their own music.

At the same time, it is striking to see how the same types of instrument occur in all the continents of the world. Making music is a very important activity. It brings people together in a unique way, and it is easy to see how musicians have shared their secrets and spread ideas from country to country.

In this book you will find examples of many different kinds of instrument, as well as maps to show where each one comes from. These instruments represent only a fraction of the rich variety in the world. If you would like to know more, there is a list of helpful books and suppliers at the back of the book.

We have shown many different methods for making the instruments, beginning with the simplest and going on to the more complex. Most of the steps are very easy to follow, but where you see this sign ask for help from an adult.

Of course, musical instruments are not just decorative. They have to work. You will need patience and perseverance both to make them and to learn how to play them well. As you become more confident, add colours, decorations and modifications of your own. In this way musicians have developed new versions of old favourites.

Music to entertain

Music making is a wonderful way of bringing people together, and you can gain much enjoyment from entertaining others. When you have made some instruments and have become reasonably good at playing them, you might like to gather a group of family or friends together to form an orchestra or band (see page 29).

Originally published as World Crafts: Musical Instruments

This edition first published in 2002

Franklin Watts
96 Leonard Street, London EC2A 4XD

Franklin Watts Australia
56 O'Riordan Street, Alexandria, NSW 2015

ISBN: 0 7496 4543 1 (pbk)
Dewey Decimal Classification Number 745.5

Series editor: Annabel Martin
Editor: Jane Walker
Design: Visual Image
Cover design: Chloë Cheesman/Mike Davis
Artwork: Ruth Levy
Photography: Peter Millard

A CIP catalogue record for this book is available from the British Library

Printed in Dubai

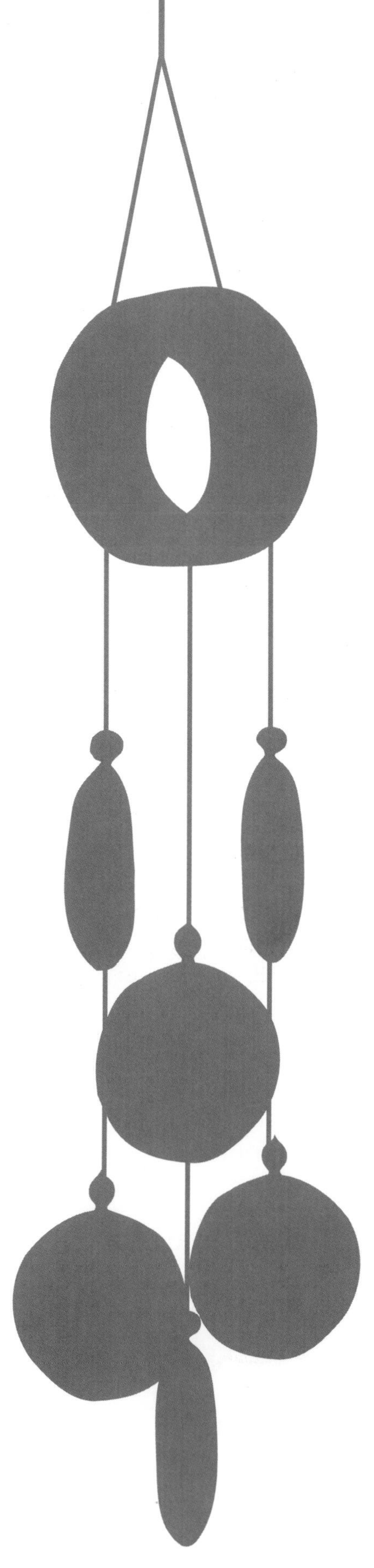

Contents

A musical history

Making music is as old as the human race itself. No-one can tell exactly when musical instruments were first used, except that people probably used themselves as instruments right from the beginning! They would clap their hands, stamp their feet and of course use their voices.

People in ancient times used natural objects to make different sounds – wood on wood, wood on stone, bone on stone. Simple rhythm instruments are known to have existed in Europe as far back as 25,000 years ago – that's around 23,000 BC!

People have also been using wind instruments for a very long time. Early flutes and horns were generally used in religious ceremonies or as a means for people to signal to one another. As civilisations became more developed in the Middle East and Europe, more sophisticated instruments were made. They began to be used for entertainment as well.

Music has been made in every culture. It is used for religious worship, important family and state occasions, parties and entertainment. Although musical styles differ from period to period and from one culture to another, the kind of instruments that people make are remarkably similar worldwide. Drums, flutes, horns, rattles and stringed instruments appear just about everywhere.

Instruments can be made simply from local materials, or by using the most complicated computer technology. All it takes to play some instruments well is a good sense of timing and rhythm, while others need years of practice. In either case, the joy that people get from playing and listening to music is equally worthwhile.

Your own music-making kit

Many of the instruments in this book are made from natural materials. Others use manufactured items like cardboard tubes, tin cans and bottle tops. Put together your own music-making kit by collecting materials you may need. Keep small items in plastic pots and the rest in a big cardboard box, together with a set of tools.

Here are some of the most useful items for your music-making kit:

hammer • tenon saw • hacksaw • vice • awl • hand drill • pliers • wood file or rasp • scissors • heavy craft knife • metal ruler • brushes • white emulsion • poster paints • varnish • PVA (white) glue • tube of strong glue • plastic modelling material • modelling clay • wood • dowel • wire • leather • bamboo • string • masking tape • paper • pen • pencil • felt pens • needle and thread • metal skewer • nails • wooden block to hammer on • sandpaper • newspaper to work on • protective gloves • apron • paper towels for cleaning up

Ideas for decoration

When you have made a musical instrument you can invent your own style of decoration. Try using different colours, patterns and shapes. If the instruments come from a different culture to your own and you need some inspiration, visit your local or school library. Look for a book about the particular country or people that interest you.

See if you can find the different ways in which they decorate the things they make.

Trace patterns and shapes, or adapt them freely for your own use. We have used this method for the prayer drum on page 25. The design was taken from one sewn in beads on the back of a North American Indian baby carrier, called a cradleboard.

Sticks and stones

Rhythm is essential to making music, and clapping is one of the simplest means of keeping a beat. Some of the first musical instruments that people invented were designed to do their clapping for them! In ancient Egypt ivory clappers were made with just that purpose in mind.

We still use this method to beat out a rhythm. The modern wooden clappers shown below left are made by the Aboriginal people of Australia. They are carved from hardwood and a hot metal skewer is used to burn in the decorations.

Shakers or rattles can also be made from animal or sea shells, hide and leather, horn, wood and metal. Leg rattles like the one on the right are called *amahlwayi.* They are made from insect cocoons by the Ndebele tribe of Zimbabwe. The Mexican scraper (above), which is called a *guiro,* is sounded by running a stick along the ridges that are cut into the wood.

Instruments that make use of the sounds made by natural objects such as stone, wood or metal, are called ideophones. They can be played by stamping with the feet, shaking, rattling, hitting with another object, banging or scraping together, or plucking.

Make your own rhythm sticks

You will need: 40 cm dowel • saw • vice • sandpaper • wood file or rasp • protective gloves • metal meat skewer • pliers • poster paints • varnish

Can you think of other ideas for sound-makers? Gently tap as many things as you can find with a dowel beater. Be careful not to try anything fragile. Most materials have a natural note when sounded. Here are some suggestions: milk bottles (the note can be altered by pouring in some water), saucepan lids, radiators, waste bins, tiles, a nail hung on a string, wooden floorboards and tin trays.

1 Grip dowel in vice and saw off two 20-cm lengths.

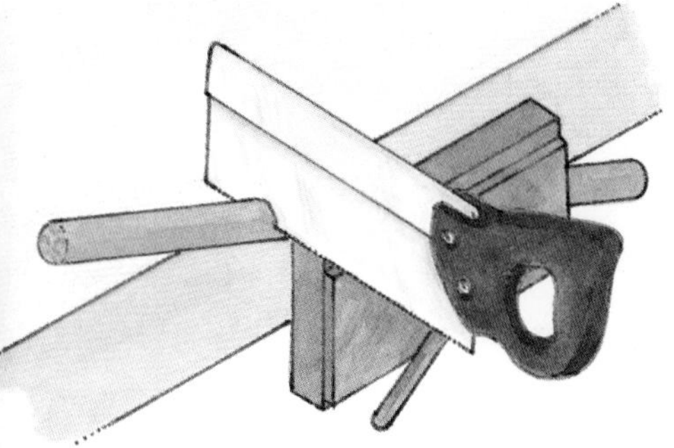

2 Smooth ends with sandpaper or shape to a point with file or rasp.

3 To decorate sticks Aboriginal style, put on protective gloves. Grip skewer in pliers and hold in a gas flame until very hot. Lay hot skewer across wood in vice so that it burns a brown mark. The end of the skewer makes a round dot.

Repeat, making more marks, to form pattern. When finished, run cold water over skewer to cool it.

4 Alternatively, you can decorate your sticks by painting and varnishing them.

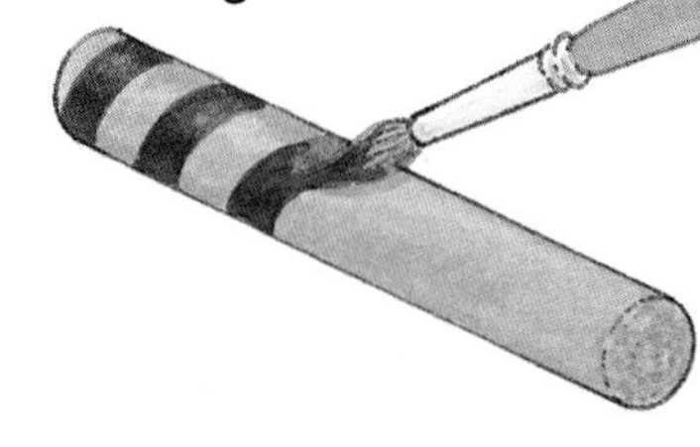

You could make a *guiro* scraper by wrapping and tying string around a large plastic bottle. Then scrape it with a stick.

Shake and rattle

When a gourd or a seed pod dries in the sun, the flesh shrivels up leaving the hard seeds to rattle around inside. These natural rattles have long been used in music and magical rituals. The black gourd rattle from Southern Africa (right) is a good example.

A gourd is also the basis for the *kass-kassa* (sometimes called a *shekere* or *kabassa*). The one shown top right is made by Issifou Amadou in Togo. The calabash gourds are specially grown and trained to the correct shape. The covering is made from elephant grass seeds threaded on a string mesh. The shaker is held in the hand and the seeds are shaken against the surface or swirled around the gourd.

The hand-made *tioco-tioco-ni* (pronounced 'chiko-chiko-ni'), or basketwork shaker (above left), has a gourd or tin base. The seeds rattle against it. The shaker is obviously modelled on the shape of a gourd.

Weave a basket shaker

You will need: pair of compasses • cork tile • awl • newspaper • craft knife • 38-cm lengths of cane • string or raffia • ball • dried chick peas or beans • masking tape

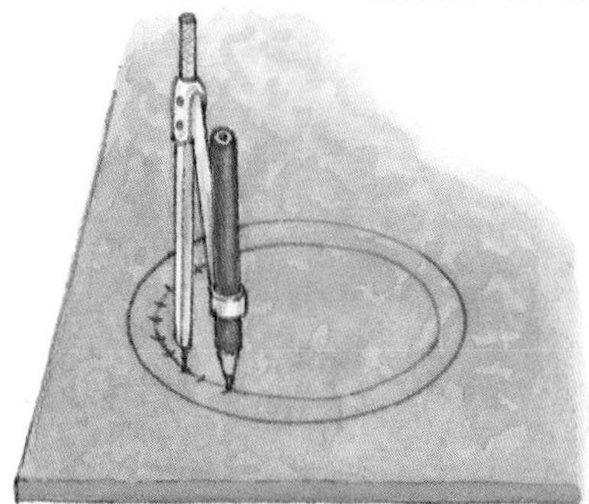

1 Use compasses to draw two circles, radius 3.6 and 4.6 cm, on cork tile. Set compasses to 1 cm apart and divide inner circle into 23 sections.

2 Lay tile on newspaper. Cut around outer circle with craft knife. Make hole at each point on inner circle with awl.

3 Soak cane in water until pliable. Push 5 cm of each cane through each hole in the cork circle. Weave ends of cane together around base as shown.

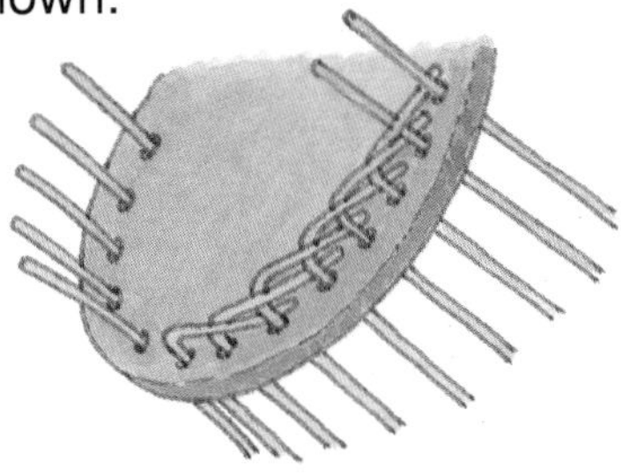

4 On top side, tie end of string or raffia to base of a cane. Weave in and out, pushing string down as you go. Use different colours to build up stripes. Encourage your work to bend outwards by putting a ball inside canes.

5 After 6 cm of weaving, remove ball and begin to draw weaving inwards towards a point. Before closing rattle completely, drop in a handful of dried chick peas or beans.

6 Divide ends of canes into two bunches and form into a circular handle. Secure with masking tape. Bind handle with string or raffia.

Handy hint: If craft cane is not available, buy a small basket at a charity shop and unravel it.

Bells on their toes

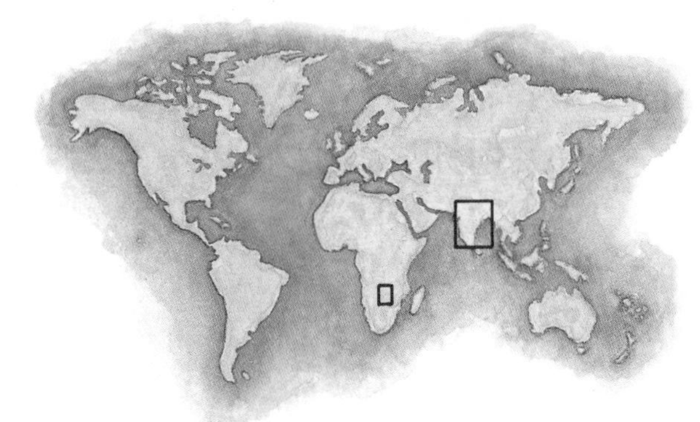

Bells and jingles are examples of metal ideophones. Bells have a loose 'clapper', which hits against the metal sides. They are often used by dancers because they emphasise the body's movements.

The *ghungaroo* (right) are brass dancing bells from India. They can be worn around the ankle, wrist or waist on a string or belt. Morris dancers in Britain use similar bells for their dances.

Metal jingles, which are similar to bells, have a long history in dance and as an aid to prayer and worship. The *sistrum,* which is a metal and wire shaker, can be traced back to ancient Egypt and Roman Pompeii. It is used today by the Coptic church of Ethiopia. The wooden *sistrum* below comes from Harare, Zimbabwe. It is made with recycled bottle-tops.

The tambourine above is also from Harare. Tambourines, or frame drums, originated in the Middle East.

Make a cake tin tambourine

You could make a *sistrum* from a branch with its bark removed. Use the same method as for the tambourine shown here. Put the branch in a vice and drill holes for the wire. Decorate using a hot skewer (see page 7), or paint and varnish.

You will need: small shallow cake tin • tin opener • hammer • wooden block • file • felt pen • awl • heavy craft knife • bottle tops • pliers • plastic modelling material • coathanger wire

1 Remove base of tin with tin opener.

Hammer rough edges flat on wooden block. Smooth with file.

2 Mark a rectangle, 5 x 2.5 cm, on side of tin. Add a line down the centre of the rectangle. Repeat at 5-cm intervals until you have five rectangles.

3 Punch hole with awl halfway down each side of each rectangle as shown.

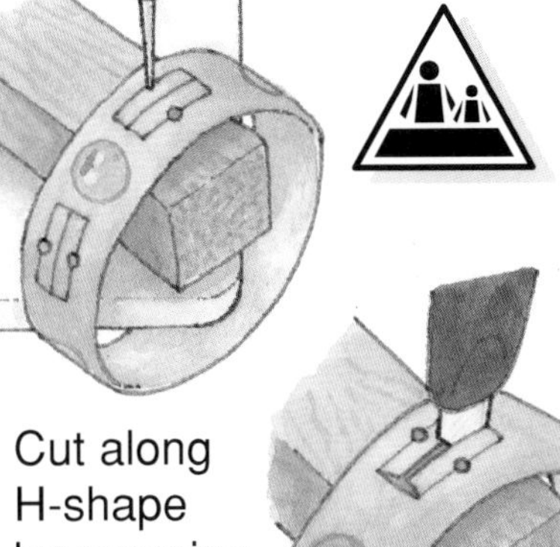

Cut along H-shape by pressing on tin with heavy craft knife.

4 Hold each bottle top in pliers and beat flat with hammer on wooden block.

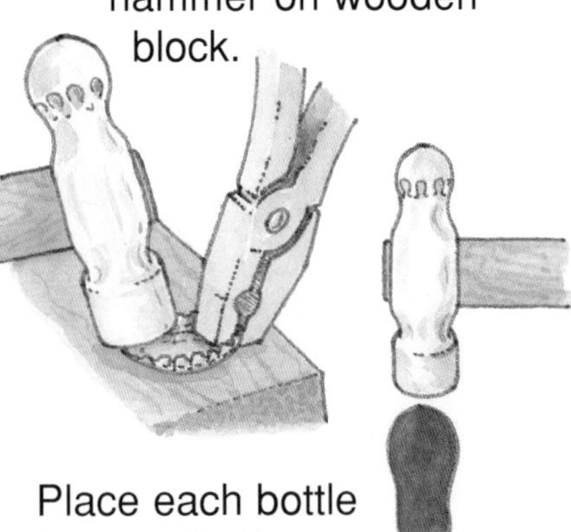

Place each bottle top on plastic modelling material and punch hole in centre with awl.

5 Cut 5 pieces of wire, 5 cm long. On inside of tin, bend back two sides of rectangles, to form tabs.

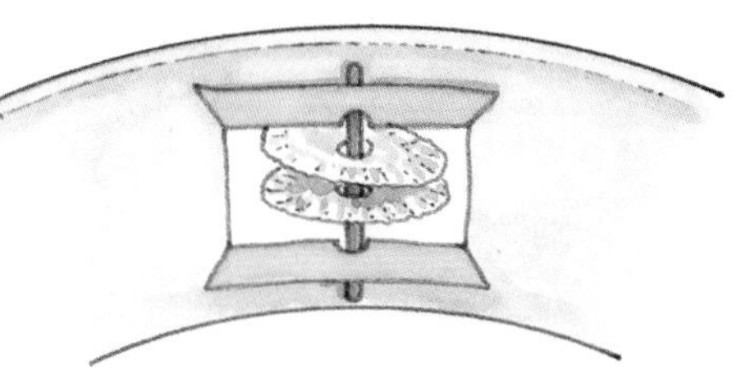

6 Thread wire through one hole, two bottle tops and second hole. Flatten tin tabs with hammer, to hold wire in place. Flatten sharp edges.

Hanging sounds

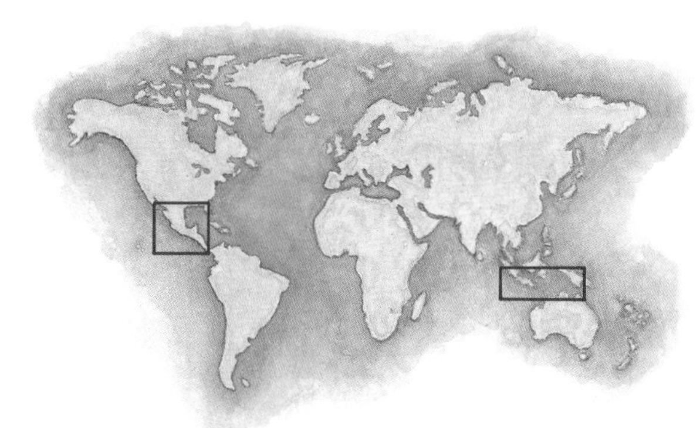

Wind chimes like these ones from Mexico are another form of ideophone. Natural objects like wood, stone or fired clay have their own particular tone if suspended and allowed to vibrate freely. Try this for yourself. Tie a piece of cotton around a nail. Hold the nail up so that it does not touch anything else, then hit it with a dowel. It should make a ringing sound. Different-sized nails make different notes.

This same principle is also used by the family of instruments which includes the xylophone (wooden bars), the lithophone (stone or slate) and the metalophone (metal). The bars are suspended above tubes or gourds that act as sound boxes.

Highly developed bar ideophones are found in the *gamelan* orchestras of Java and Bali in Indonesia. These orchestras provide music for shadow puppet plays. Instruments in the *gamelan* include large gongs, which are suspended in decorated frames, and the *gender*, or wooden xylophone (right).

Make tile music

If you have access to clay and a kiln, you could make fired-clay bars for your *gender*. Otherwise, the edging pieces used in tiling work very well.

You will need: cereal packet • scissors • five toilet roll tubes • strong glue • a length of wooden batten, 1.5 x 1.5 cm • pencil • 12 2-cm nails with flat heads • white emulsion • poster paints • varnish • five tile edging pieces • pliers • 10 small rubber bands

1 Cut cereal packet to same height as cardboard tubes. Glue tubes to inside of packet.

2 Cut two wooden battens the same length as cereal packet. Hold battens alongside tubes. Mark dots at either end and between tubes. Knock nail into wood at each dot, leaving 1.5 cm of each nail sticking up.

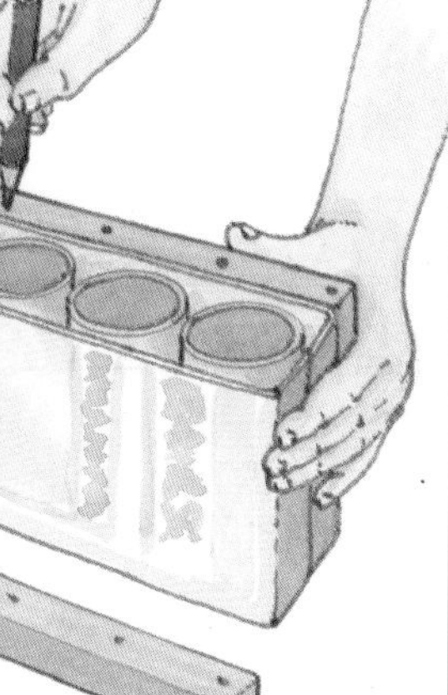

3 Glue battens along top edges of box. Glue base of box to two short battens as feet. Paint with white emulsion, decorate with poster paints and varnish.

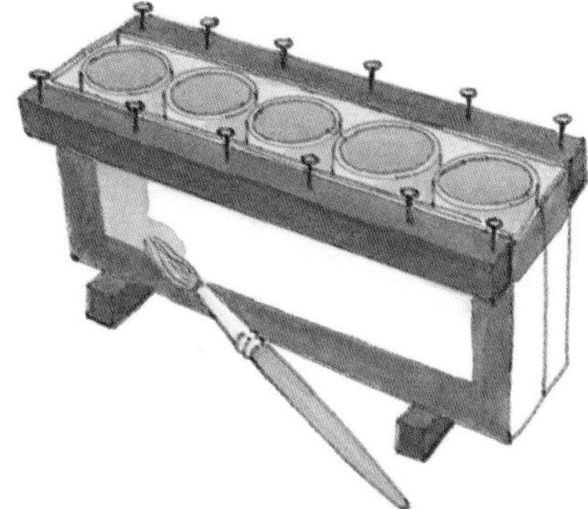

4 Keep one tile at full length. Shorten the next bar by gently breaking 1 cm off one end with a pair of pliers. Shorten the next by 2 cm and so on until fifth bar is 4 cm shorter. (Be careful to wrap and throw away sharp pieces of tile.)

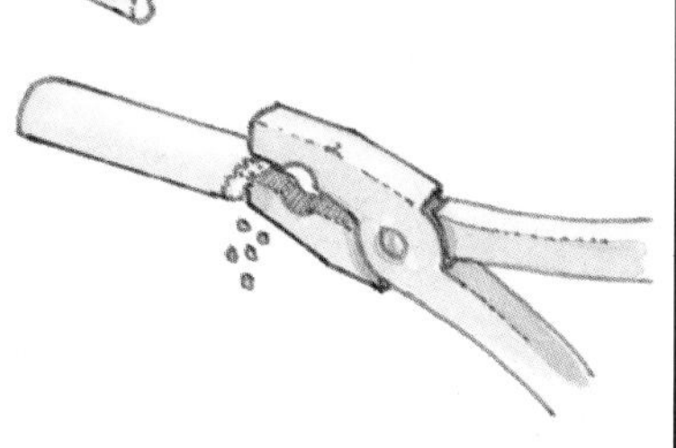

5 Stretch rubber bands between each nail along batten on both sides. Suspend bars by twisting rubber bands and pushing bars between them along length of instrument as shown. Check note of each bar with a piano. Tune by removing a little more tile.

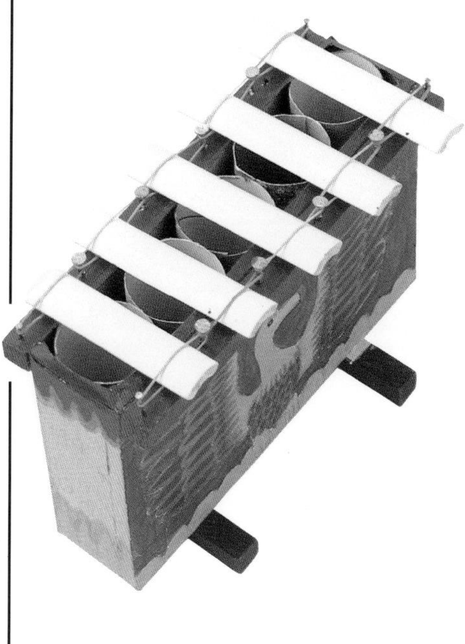

PAKISTAN & KENYA

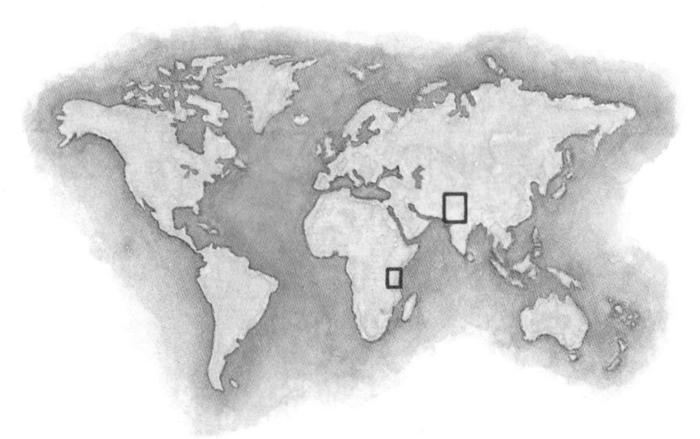

'Tongues' and thumbs

These instruments belong to the linguaphone family (from *lingua*, the Latin word for 'tongue'). Sounds from the vibrating 'tongue' are amplified by directing them into a confined space called a sound box, or resonator.

The jew's (or jaw's) harp works by plucking a 'tongue' which is held between two sides of a frame. The frame is placed between the player's teeth. The open mouth is the resonator and the pitch of the note is changed by moving the player's tongue or cheeks. This man from Pakistan is playing a jaw's harp.

The *mbira, sansa* or 'thumb piano' originated in Africa. This one is from Kenya. It is held in the palms of the hands and the thumbs are used to pluck the 'tongues'. They are held tightly against a bridge on a piece of wood or a box. Often the wood is carved, painted and decorated. Extra rattling sounds can be added by wrapping wire around the tongues, or by nailing flattened bottle tops to the box.

Make a thumb piano

You need a length of bamboo cane to make a bamboo jaw's harp. Split the cane in half with a craft knife. Make two more cuts, leaving a tongue in between. Hold the harp in your teeth and pluck the tongue to make a note.

You will need: a piece of wooden board, 20 x 1.5 x 12 cm • pencil • ruler • V-shaped linoleum cutting tool • dark-brown shoe polish • polishing cloth • pliers • coathanger wire • hammer • 10 metal staples

1 Draw two lines 3 and 4.5 cm from end of board. Mark a pattern of lines on rest of surface. Carve pattern into wood with linoleum cutting tool. (Always work away from your hands.)

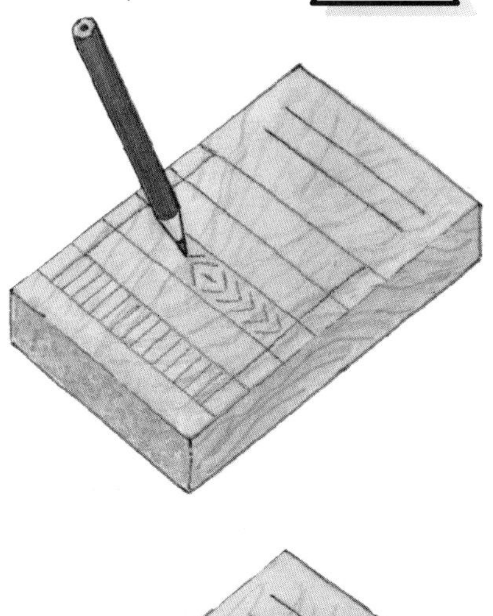

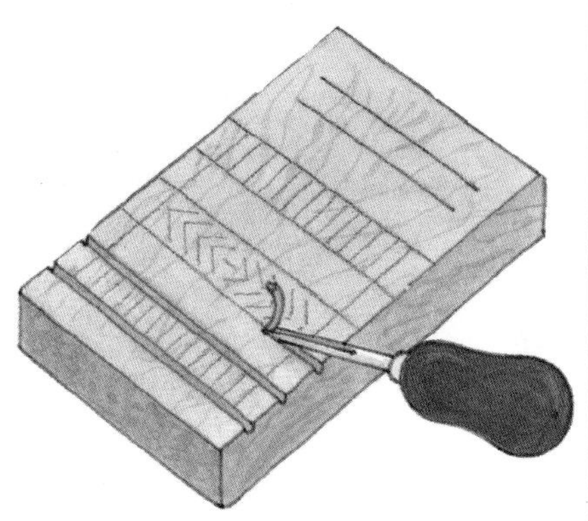

2 Polish wood with dark-brown shoe polish. Rub off excess polish.

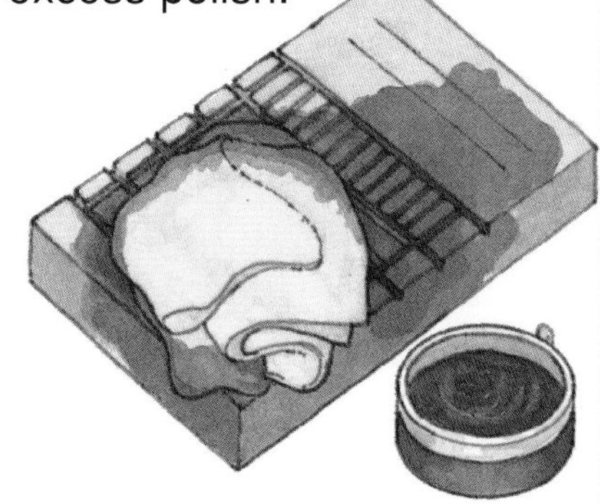

3 Cut seven pieces of coathanger wire of different lengths, from 12 to 9 cm. Hold each one over a very hard surface with pliers. Beat ends flat with hammer. Cut two more pieces of wire 10 cm long.

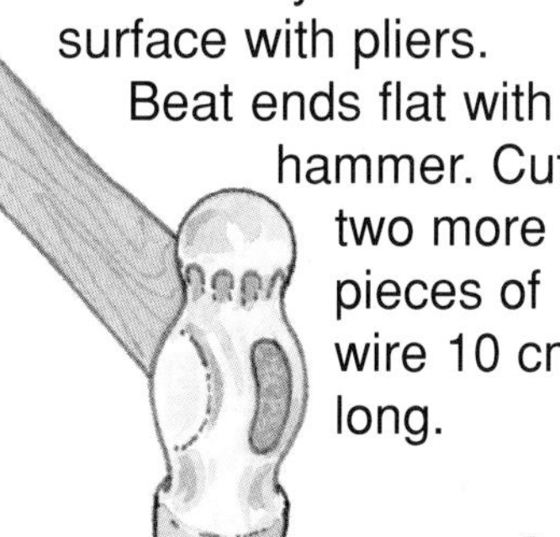

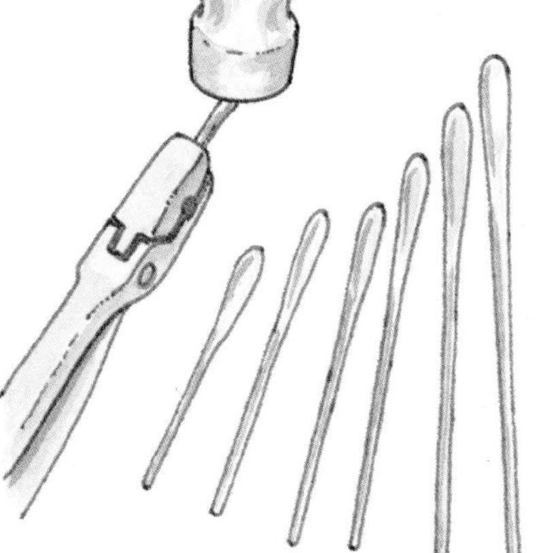

4 Lay one piece of 10-cm wire along second line on wood and hammer in staple at each end. Lay all 7 tongues across this wire. Lay second piece of wire over tongues along first line. Staple at both ends and between each tongue. Check that tongues make a good, clear sound.

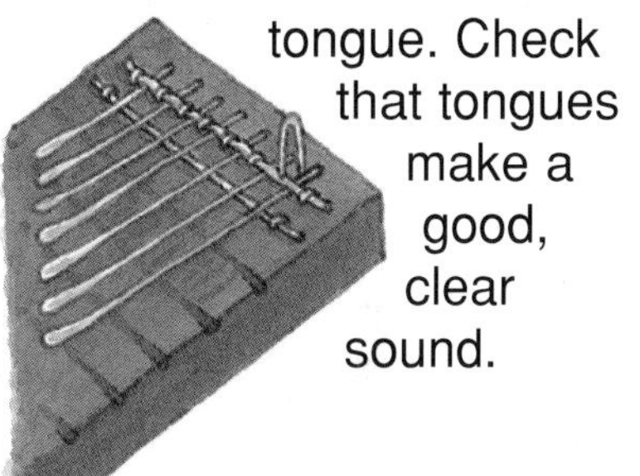

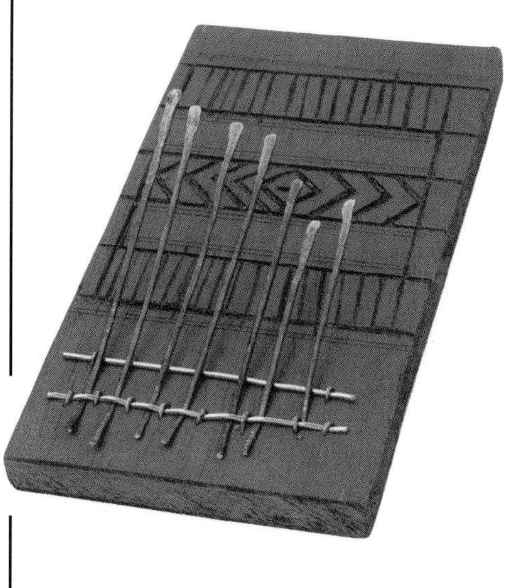

Central America, Mozambique & Peru

Flutes and whistles

Long ago, people discovered that they could make pleasant sounds by blowing air against a sharp edge. This caused the air to vibrate. The musical instruments that use this principle are called aerophones. They range from simple penny whistles to the grandest church organ.

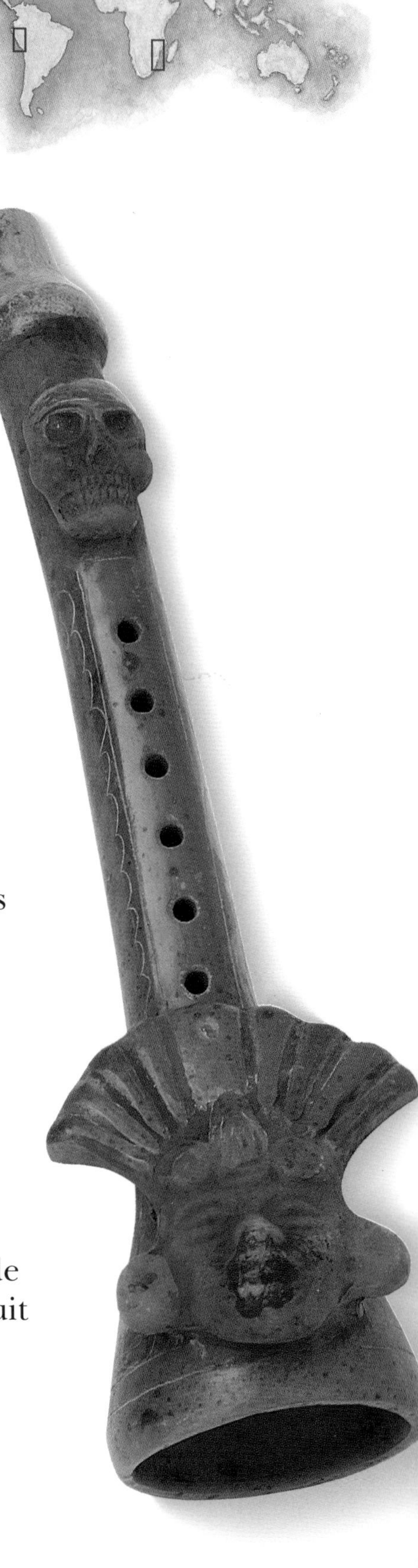

Bird bone whistles and flutes have been found dating back to the Stone Age. The Andean Indians of South America believed that playing flutes made from the bones of your enemies gave you power over them. The ceramic flute (right) is a copy of one made by the Mayan peoples of Central America some 2,000 years ago. It is very similar to the recorder which is played in schools today. The little bird whistle above is from Costa Rica.

A sound can also be made by blowing over a hole in a round or shaped vessel. You can change the note by covering and uncovering other holes with your fingers. The round vessel flute (top left) works on this principle. It is made from a dried matamba fruit in Mozambique. The decorated ceramic flute (left), called an ocarina, comes from Peru.

Make a clay flute

You will need: modelling clay • knife • large needle • poster paints • varnish

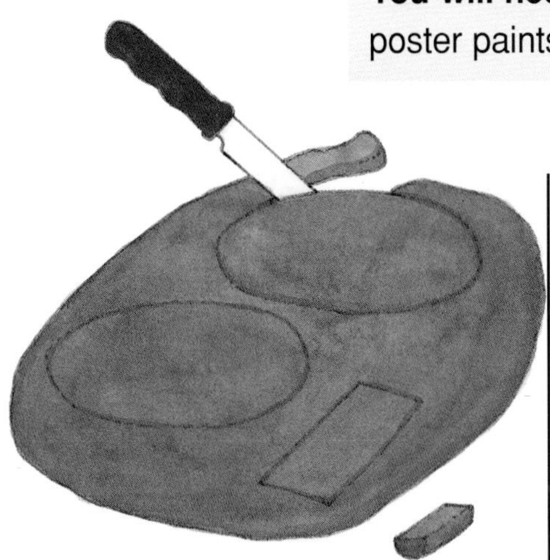

1 Roll a piece of clay flat. Cut out two egg shapes, 7 cm across and 9 cm long, and a rectangle 5 x 2 cm. Make a roll of clay 2 cm long. Cut thin slice off side of roll.

2 Score edges of each clay piece with large needle and moisten with water. Form each egg into a bowl shape. Press the two shapes carefully together to form a hollow egg. Score edges together with needle, leaving gap at one end. Smooth join with a little water.

3 Form clay rectangle into short tube and attach it to egg by scoring. Push clay roll into tube, flat side up, leaving a gap to blow through. Smooth clay with dampened fingers.

4 Use needle to make four small holes in upper surface of egg shape. Make one larger hole on top, just behind blowing hole.

Make two small holes in lower surface.

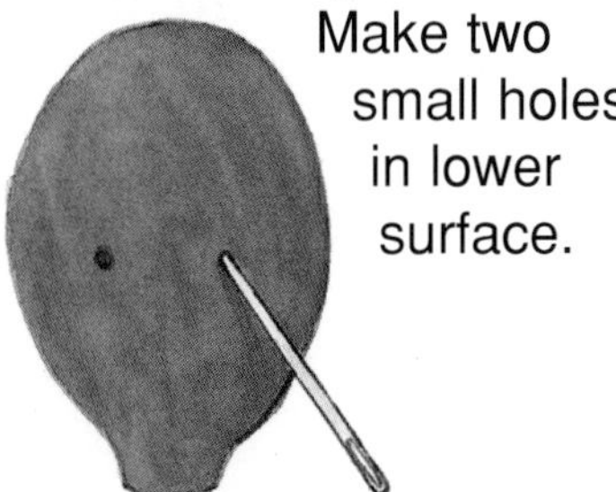

5 Check flute works before it dries hard. Cover four small holes with fingers and gently blow through end hole.

If flute does not whistle, adjust the edge of large hole. (The sound is made by blown air hitting the far edge of this hole.)

6 Leave to dry. Paint and varnish.

Pipes to blow

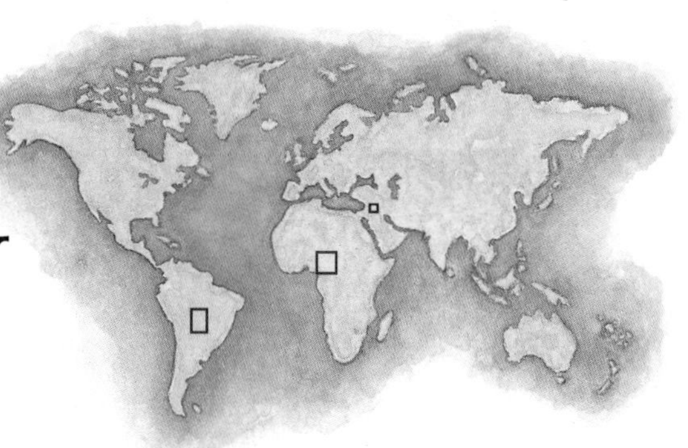

Many instruments have developed from the simple idea of blowing down a tube. The South American *zamponas* shown below are probably the best known. They are sometimes called panpipes because the Greek god Pan was always shown playing them. *Zamponas* are made up of small flutes that are crafted from bamboo grown in Bolivia. The flutes are joined together in a row. They have no finger holes and are closed at one end.

Trumpets and horns are larger versions of the pipe. They are played by vibrating the lips together and using the pipe as the resonator. Horns, as their name suggests, were originally made from animal horns. Trumpets were made from any material that could be hollowed out, such as wood, bamboo, bark or metal. The decorated gourd horn shown left is from Nigeria.

Another group of pipes uses a thin tongue, called a reed, to vibrate the air. The clarinet, oboe, bassoon and bagpipes come into this category. The double clarinet below is from Syria.

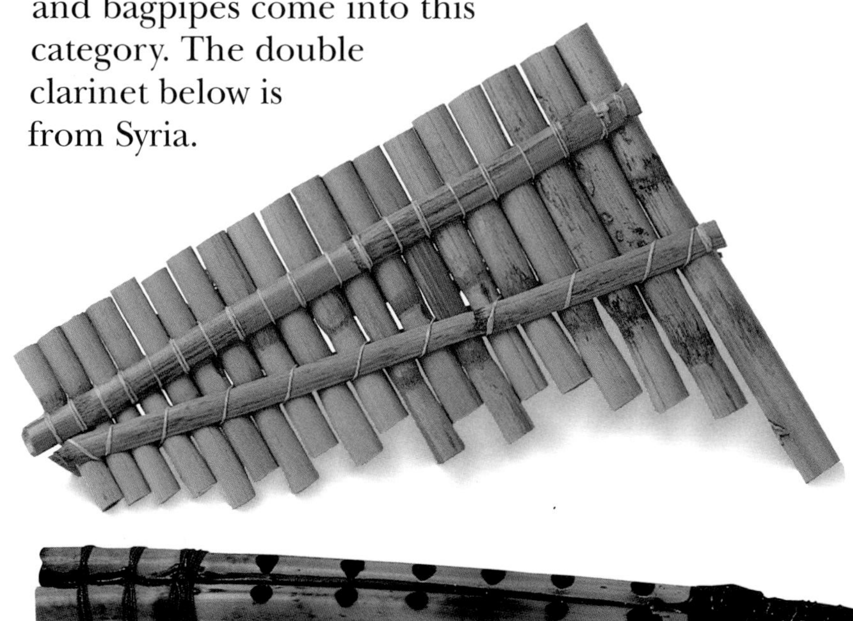

Make some panpipes

This set of eight pipes will give you a scale of G major. You will need to tune each pipe as you make it, using a piano or recorder (see page 29). If the pipe sounds too low (flat), saw some more off its length. If it is too high (sharp), use it for the next pipe and make a new, longer one.

You will need: 1.5-cm garden bamboo cane, at least 8 sections long • vice • saw • sandpaper • pea stick • ruler • pencil • heavy craft knife • thick cotton or twine

1 Grip garden cane in vice and cut into 8 sections just below each knot in bamboo. Remove pith from inside tubes with rolled-up sandpaper.

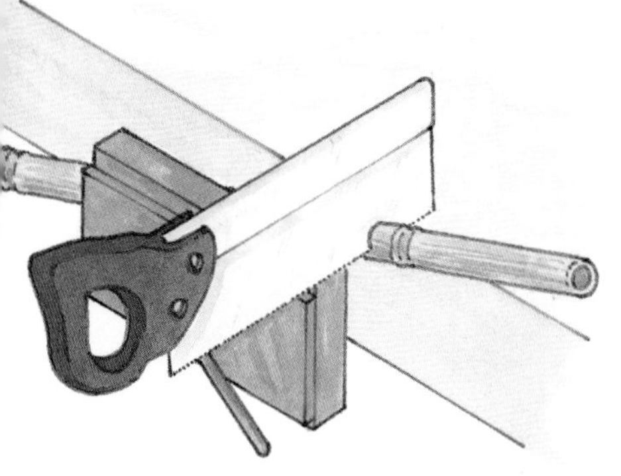

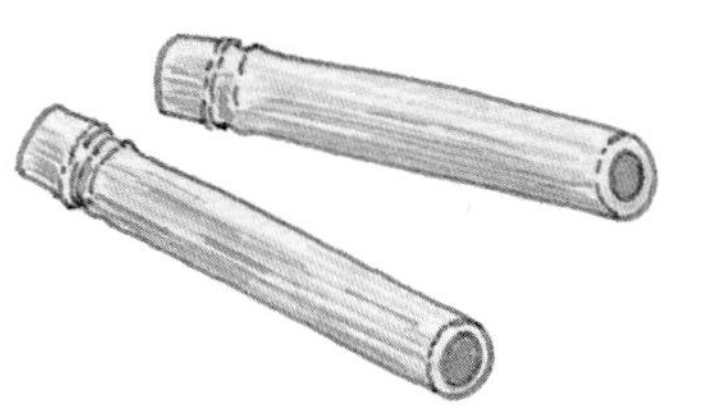

2 Use a pea stick as a gauge. Measure 107 mm from one end and make a mark. Push it down inside bamboo tube and mark length. Remove and hold alongside bamboo with length mark in place. Transfer 107-mm mark to bamboo. Shorten bamboo to this mark with saw.

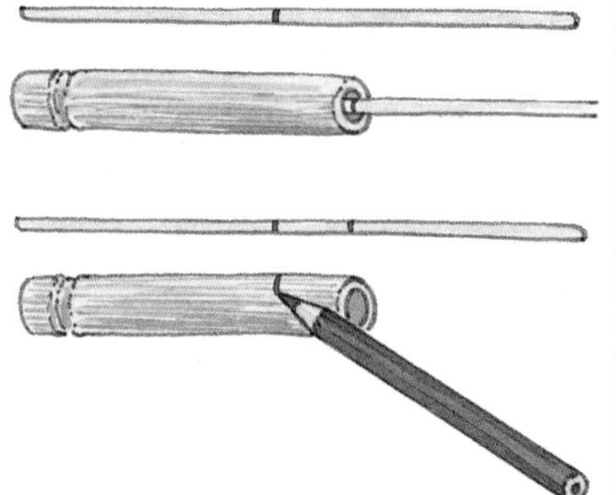

3 Repeat this process, with the other 7 pipes, marking them at 94, 82, 77, 69, 61, 56 and 49 mm. Sand pipes until smooth and check notes (see above).

4 Cut another piece of bamboo, 14 cm long, with no knots. Split in half with heavy craft knife.

5 Tie length of thick cotton or twine around longest pipe. Lash diagonally to half bamboo strip, wind around top and on to next pipe. Continue until all eight pipes are held firmly in place. Knot end of twine.

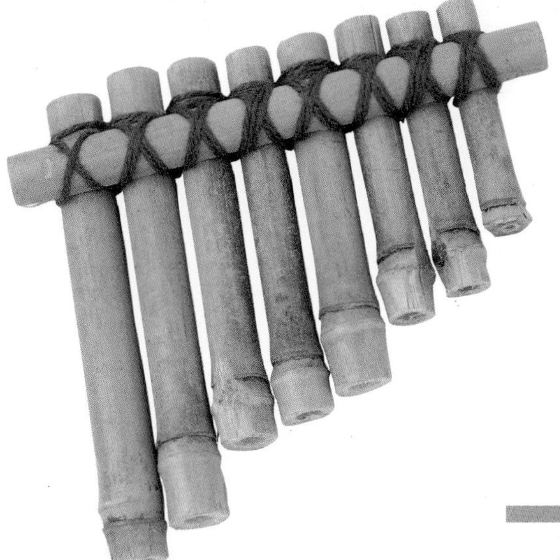

Strings and bows

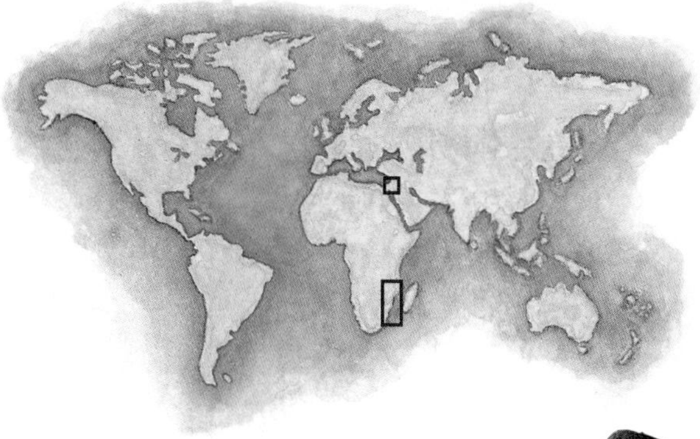

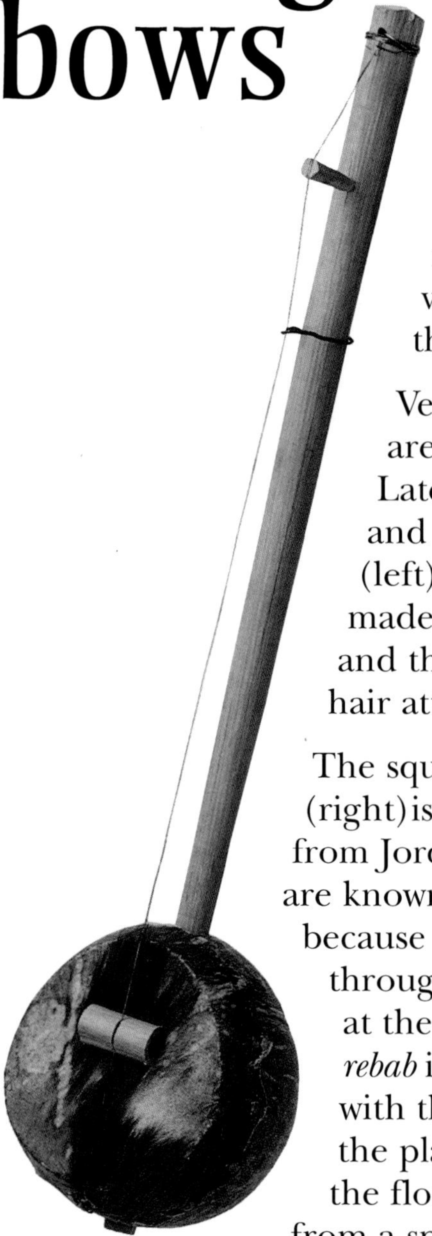

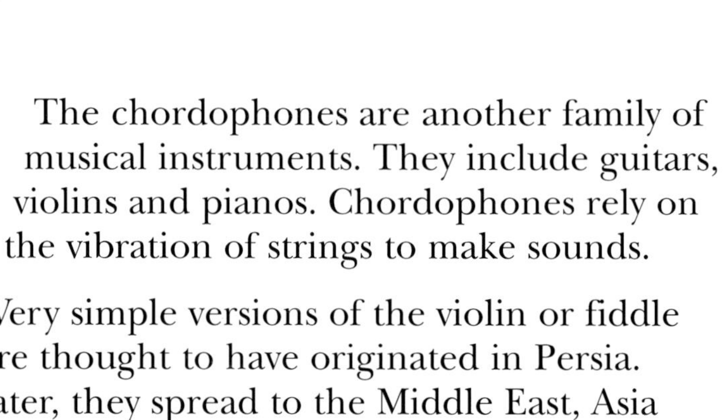

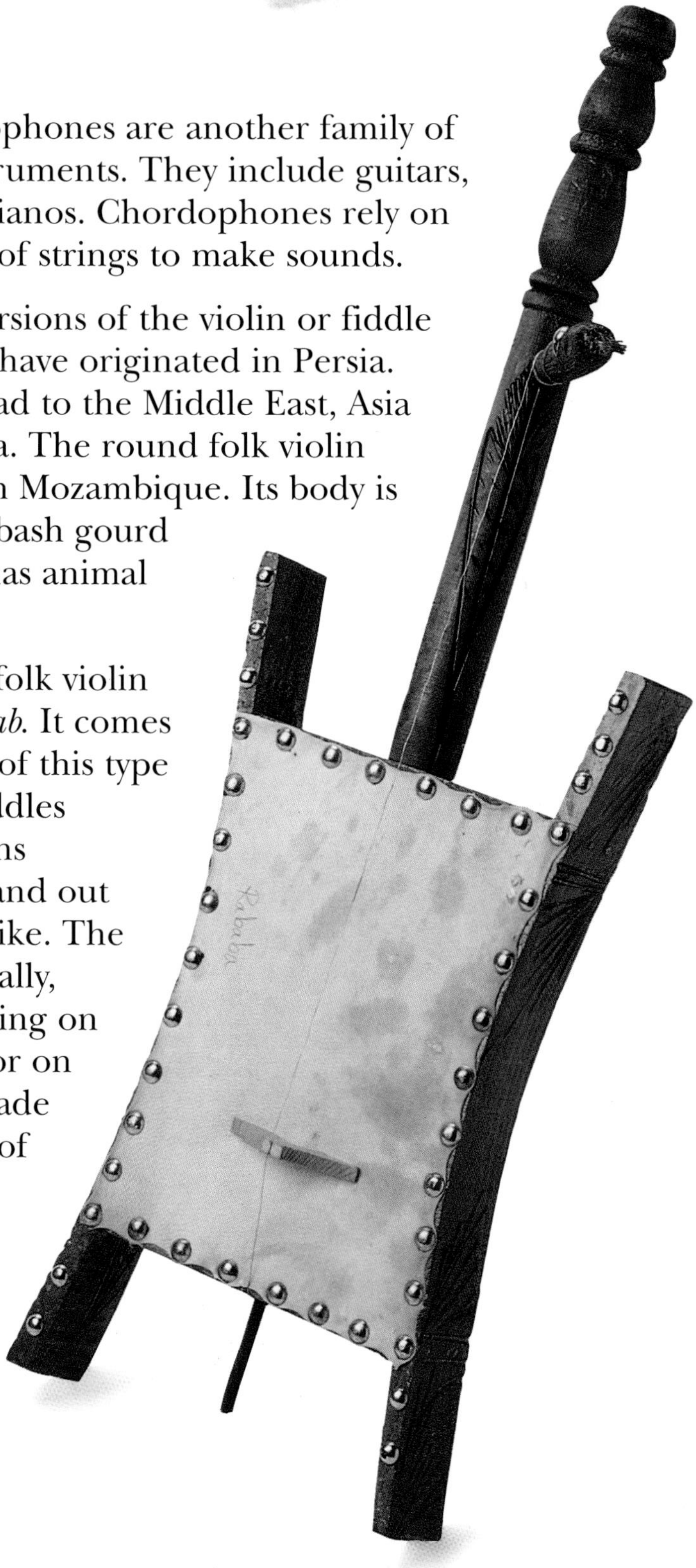

The chordophones are another family of musical instruments. They include guitars, violins and pianos. Chordophones rely on the vibration of strings to make sounds.

Very simple versions of the violin or fiddle are thought to have originated in Persia. Later, they spread to the Middle East, Asia and North Africa. The round folk violin (left) comes from Mozambique. Its body is made from a calabash gourd and the skin still has animal hair attached to it.

The square-shaped folk violin (right)is called a *rebab.* It comes from Jordan. Violins of this type are known as spike fiddles because the neck runs through the body and out at the base as a spike. The *rebab* is held vertically, with the spike resting on the player's knee or on the floor. A bow made from a springy piece of wood is drawn across the string to play the instrument.

Make a one-string violin

This instrument is played by running a bow across the string to vibrate it. (See page 28 for instructions on making a bow.) You can change the note by pressing your finger on the neck end of the string.

You will need: coconut • skewer • plastic modelling material • protective gloves • saw • knife • sandpaper • vice • hand drill • 1-cm dowel, 47 cm long • chamois leather • pencil • carpet tacks • stick • craft knife • guitar string or fuse wire • small bamboo ring • thin garden cane • string

1 Use the skewer to pierce two coconut 'eyes' (flat areas near the point of the nut). Let milk drain out. Stand nut on plastic modelling material. Using protective gloves, hold nut firmly and ask an adult to saw it in half lengthways.

2 Remove flesh from one half with a knife. Sand the outside of shell smooth.

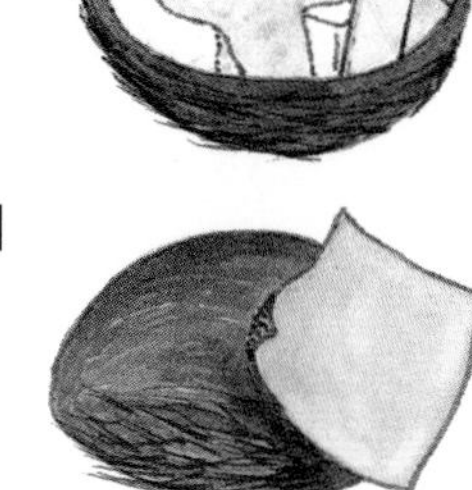

3 Grip shell in vice and drill row of small holes 1 cm from edge all round. Drill 1-cm hole at both ends of shell. Drill small hole 1 cm from end of dowel and a larger one 7 cm from same end.

4 Draw around nut on chamois leather. Cut out shape 2 cm larger. Soak leather in water, squeeze out and stretch over shell to form drum. Hammer tacks into small holes, stretching leather across nut. Trim off excess leather. Allow to dry.

5 Push dowel through two large holes so that end sticks out 3 cm. Whittle peg from stick and score groove across top. Push peg into larger hole. Thread guitar string through small hole, around dowel several times and over groove in peg. Pull tight and tie around dowel spike. Add tension to wire by adding bridge made from grooved bamboo ring.

CHINA & ZIMBABWE

Guitars old and new

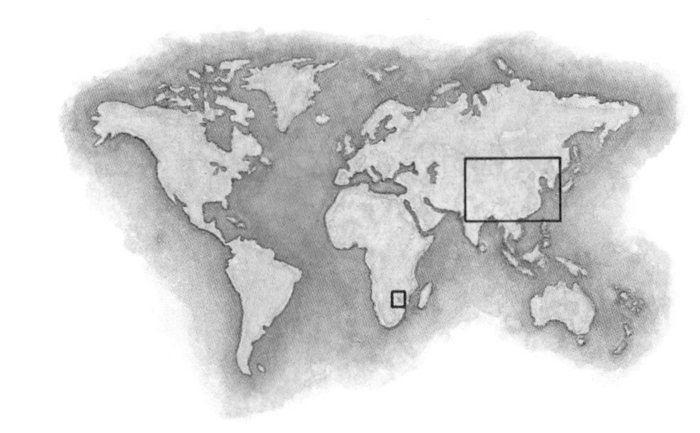

The modern-day guitar is closely related to the family of lutes and mandolins that have been popular all over the world for many hundreds of years. The Chinese *p'i p'a* (shown right) has been in existence for at least 2,000 years, and the Japanese *biwa* developed from it. This family of instruments has grown to include the European *bouzouki, tambura, balilaika* and *bandoura,* and the Middle Eastern *ud, tambur* and *rar.* In India the *sitar* and *surbahar* from the north, and the *tambura* and *mayuri* from the south, are all related.

The *ramkie* is a simple folk guitar from Southern Africa. The one shown above comes from Harare, Zimbabwe. It is made from an old oil can.

Recycle an oil can

You will need: large, square-shaped oil can • awl • hammer • heavy craft knife • detergent • two pieces of wood, 1.5 x 6 x 75 cm and 1 x 1.5 x 6 cm • sandpaper • wood file or rasp • emulsion paint • wood drill • length of stick • nails • four guitar strings • thick rubber strip

1 Drain oil from can. Punch a number of large holes in front left side of can with awl.

2 Cut around three sides of a rectangle on top right side of can with heavy craft knife. Bend tab upright. Punch four holes through side and base of can on right side. Wash out can with detergent to remove rest of oil. Leave in warm place to dry inside.

3 Use sandpaper and file or rasp to smooth wooden fingerboard. Shape and round off top corners. Drill four holes for pegs. Paint and decorate if you like.

4 Cut four 6-cm lengths of stick. Whittle into tapering pegs with craft knife. Cut a deep groove in the top of each peg. Cut four grooves into top of 6-cm wooden bridge.

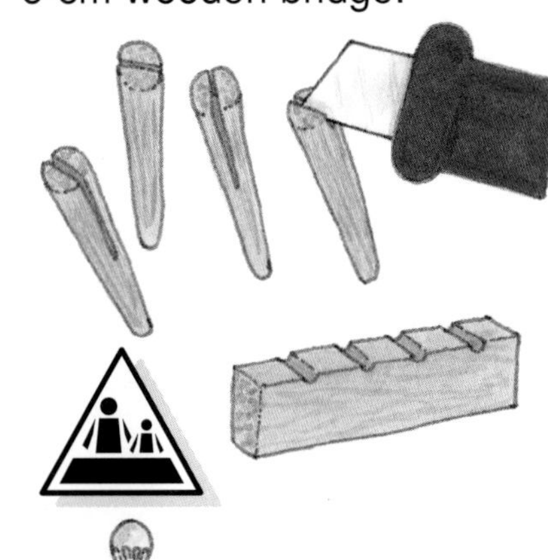

5 Slot the fingerboard into oil can and nail in place on base. Rest on edge of table and nail tab to fingerboard.

6 Tie guitar strings through holes in base and wind around pegs. Wedge pegs in holes and twist. Slip bridge under strings and rest it on can. Tune with piano or recorder.

7 To make a *capo tasto* (a device for changing the key of the strings), cut slits in both ends and middle of rubber strip. Thread a 9-cm length of stick through two slits, and lay across strings. Wrap rubber behind board and slip third slit over end of stick.

Mini drums

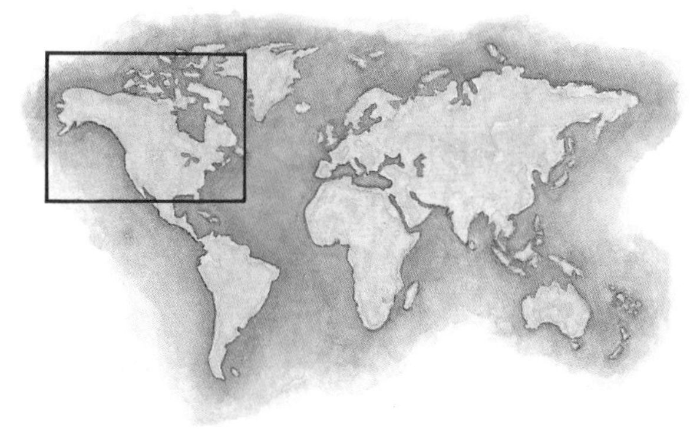

The drum family are called membranophones. The name comes from the word 'membrane', which means skin. Drums make their sound by vibrating a skin which is stretched tightly over a frame. The frame also acts as the resonator. Drums can be cylindrical (open or closed at the end), double-headed (with skins at both ends) or bowl shaped. There are a very large number of variations to these basic shapes.

The double-sided frame drum (above) is played by rotating the handle. It is sometimes called a prayer drum. Drums like this one are often associated with religious ceremonies and prayers.

The frame drum (right), with its shallow edge and double sides, may have originated in the Middle East. It is also found among the North American Indians and Inuit peoples. The tambourine (see page 11) belongs to this group of drums.

Make a paper prayer drum

This drum is simple to make from stretched paper. It is based on the same principle as the prayer drum shown opposite.

You will need: card tube, approx. 6 cm deep and 11 cm across • layout or copy paper • pencil • scissors • awl • paintbrush handle • 1.5-cm dowel, 32 cm long • strong glue • poster paint • PVA glue thinned with water • thick cotton • two small beads • drawing pins • feathers or streamers

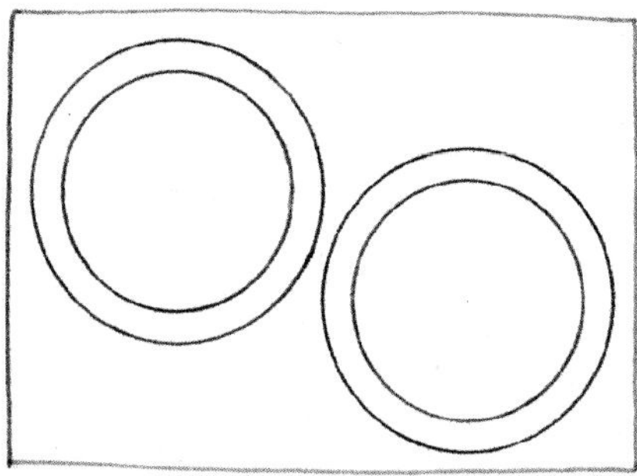

1 Draw around card tube twice on layout or copy paper. Cut two circles 3 cm larger than tube.

2 Use awl to make 1.5-cm hole in one side of card tube. Enlarge hole by pushing tapered paintbrush handle into it. Slot dowel through hole and glue to opposite side.

3 Draw and paint design on each paper circle (see page 5). Make scissor cuts all around from edge to inside circle. Paint front and back of paper discs with glue mixture.

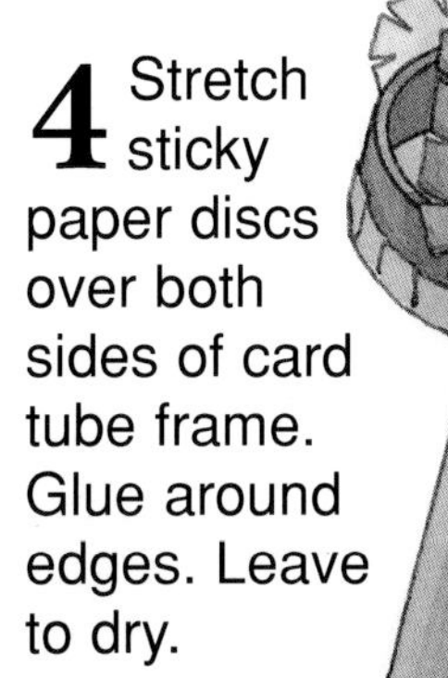

4 Stretch sticky paper discs over both sides of card tube frame. Glue around edges. Leave to dry.

5 Cut two lengths of thick cotton about 7 cm long. Tie a bead on one end. Attach cotton to either side of drum with drawing pins. Decorate with feathers or streamers.

KENYA, GAMBIA, ZIMBABWE & TUNISIA

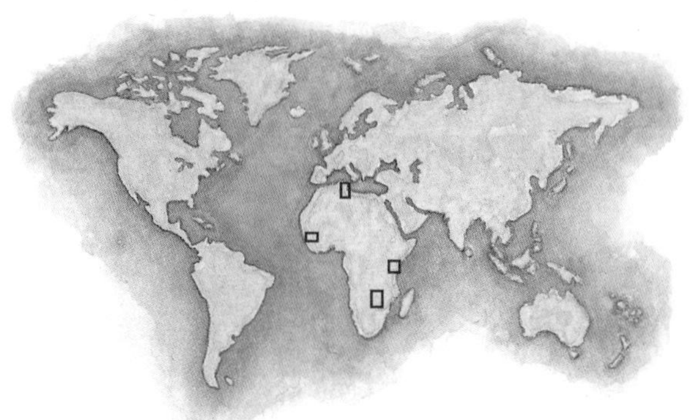

Great drums

Drums are often associated with Africa, where they play a very important role. Master drummers provide entertainment and accompaniment for dancing.

The conical *ntenga* drum (shown back right) is from Kenya. It is double-headed, but only the larger head is played. *Ntenga* are usually played in pairs of different sizes. The head and stretchers are made from animal skin. A pattern is made by twisting skin stretchers of different-coloured fur.

The large waisted drum (below left) comes from Gambia. It is made from hollowed-out wood and animal skin secured by wooden pegs. The smaller, African drum (below centre) is a 'footed' type, cut from a dried gourd. The double-headed *chigubhu* from Zimbabwe (second from left) is worn around the player's neck so that both ends can be played.

Goblet-shaped pottery drums called *darabukke* come from Islamic North Africa. They are often decorated with painting or inlaid work, like the one from Tunisia shown far right.

Make a skin drum

You will need: large cardboard tube • awl • paintbrush handle • two lengths of 1-cm dowel • dark-brown wood stain • black felt pen • brown shoe polish • chamois leather • thick cord • needle and thick cotton

Uncured animal skins are usually used for drum heads because they dry hard and taut. They are difficult to find, and most music shops no longer sell them. However, chamois leather can be bought in car accessory shops and works quite well. Cardboard tubes, plastic piping, wooden barrels or plant pots make good cylindrical drums. Pottery cooking pots, coconuts or paint tins are suitable for bowl or vessel drums.

1 Make two holes opposite each other in tube, using awl and paintbrush handle (see page 25). Push 1-cm dowel through both holes so that 3 cm stick out each side. Pierce second pair of holes, at right-angles to first. Make these slightly lower down, so that second dowel will push through.

2 Decorate tube by painting with dark-brown wood stain and black felt pen. Finish with brown shoe polish.

3 Cut circle of leather 3 cm bigger than tube. Soak in water and wring out. Make four evenly spaced holes in edge.

4 Place leather on top of tube. Run cord through one hole and under dowel. Repeat around other dowels. Wrap cord around tube twice. Knot to secure.

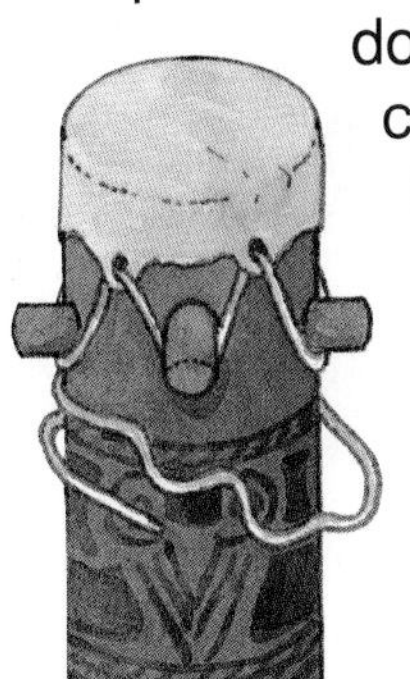

5 With needle and thick cotton, sew edge of leather to cord rings, stretching gently all around. Leave to dry.

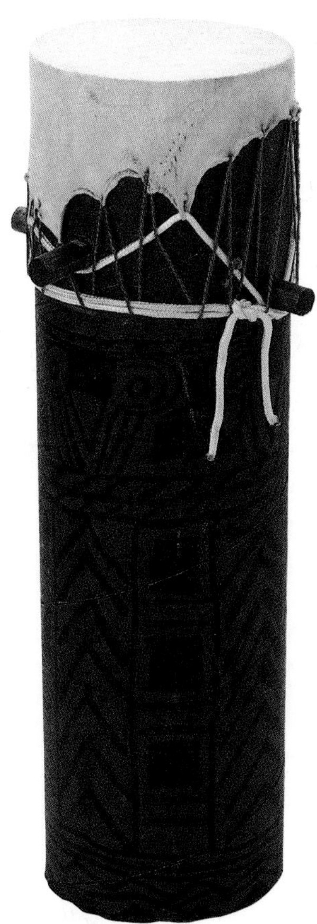

Making music

Making music together is a worldwide human activity and everywhere children are involved. They do not usually have formal lessons, but are introduced to music making from an early age.

In Africa, mothers rock their babies to sleep, singing nonsense songs which imitate drum rhythms. They carry the babies on their back to events where music is played.

American Indian children also learn music by copying. They can often reproduce a song perfectly after hearing it only once.

Teenagers are encouraged to go into the wilderness on a 'song quest' to find a tune that is uniquely their own.

In Indonesia, children learn the music of the *gamelan* orchestra by attending the puppet theatre. From around the age of five, they progress through all the instruments, playing the most difficult ones when they are adult. The most important thing in the *gamelan* orchestra is for every player to contribute to the overall sound.

Make beaters for your drums

All kinds of things can be used as beaters for drums, xylophones, etc. A knitting needle is ready to use, and a dowel can be shaped into a drumstick. Make a head for a bamboo cane from a wooden bead, a metal nut, a cork or string. Wrap masking tape around the end of a stick if you want to make a soft sound. Use brush bristles to make a rustling noise.

A bow for strings

Traditionally, the best material for a bow is horse hair that has been rubbed with resin. However, horse hair is not easy to find today. A good alternative can be nylon thread, a guitar string or stretched elastic.

Tie one end of the thread to the end of a thin garden cane. Bend the cane into a gentle arc and tie the loose end of thread to the other end.

When you have made quite a few of the instruments in this book, you may like to gather some friends together to help you make music. You could even form a band or an orchestra to entertain others.

In many cultures, music is based on the natural rhythms of speech. You can use this idea to build up a piece of music that involves as many instruments as you have available.

Begin with some words that you like; for example, 'Can you hear the music of the spheres?' Say this sentence over and over again, listening to its rhythm. Start with a steady beat (sticks/large drum/spike fiddle), then add in instruments like panpipes, guitar and *gender.* Percussion instruments (shaker/drum/tambourine) add their own rhythms. Finally, the prayer drum adds its own burst of beats.

Tuning your instruments

If you know where to find the notes of the G major and C major scales on a piano or recorder, it will help you to tune the instruments you make.

G major scale

Piano

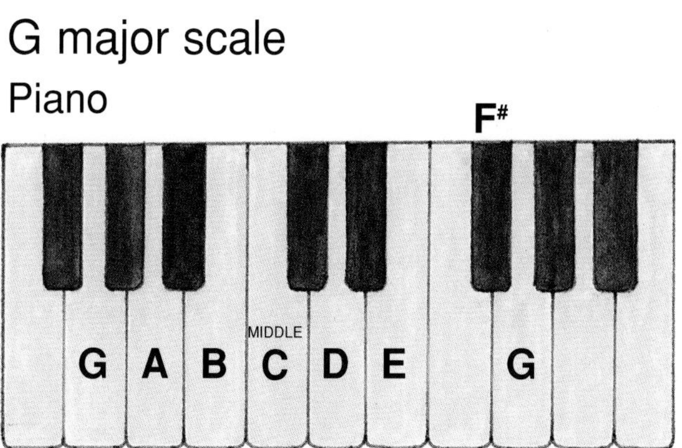

C major scale

Recorder

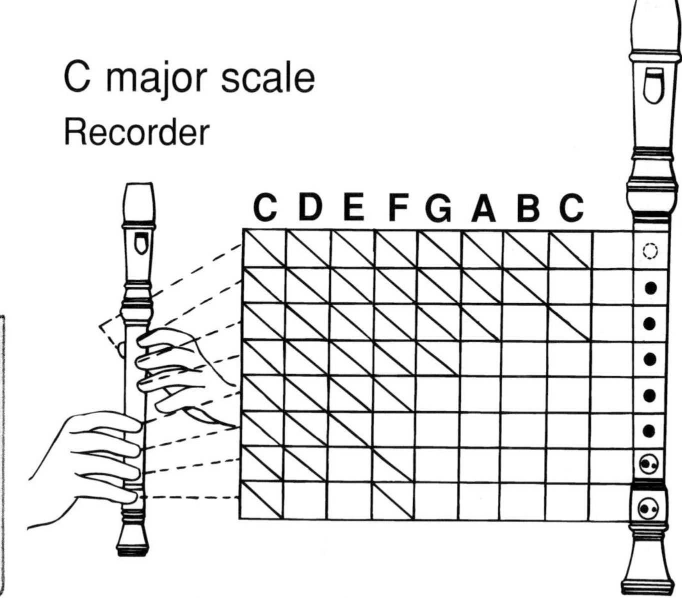

Useful information

United Kingdom

Some helpful addresses

Bangladesh Centre of
East London
185a Cannon Street Road
LONDON E1 2LX

Barnet Multicultural Study Centre
Barnet Teachers' Centre
451 High Road
Finchley
LONDON N12 0AS

Japan Information and
Cultural Centre
101–104 Piccadilly
LONDON W1V 9FN

Trishul Dance & Music Troupe
36 Airedale Road
South Ealing
LONDON W5 4SD
(Indian music workshops)

Equipment and materials

Hobby Stores
39 Parkway
LONDON NW1
(balsa wood and craft equipment)

Musical instruments for sale

Biashara
47 Colston Street
BRISTOL BS1 5AX
(world music)

Jackson Contra-Banned
Unit 2, Gatehouse Enterprise
Centre, Albert Street, Lockwood
HUDDERSFIELD HD1 3QD
(mail order catalogue and education packs)

Joliba
47 Colston Street
BRISTOL BS1 5AX
(arts from Mali & the Niger Bend – mail order catalogue and education supplement)

Kimm Barrall Design
42 Newton Drive
SAWBRIDGEWORTH
Herts CM21 9HE
(West African percussion instruments)

Knock on Wood
Granary Wharf
LEEDS LS1 4BR
(multicultural music supplies)

Oxfam Education
46a Church Street
Stoke Newington
LONDON N16 0LU
('drop-in time' Wednesdays 2–7pm)

Soma Books Ltd
38 Kennington Lane
LONDON SE11 4LS
(Indian instruments and book list)

Tumi Music Ltd & Tumi Latin
American Crafts
8–9 New Bond Street Place
BATH BA1 1BH

World Art
164 Brook Road
LONDON E5 8AP
(instruments from Zimbabwe and Southern Africa)

Books

Art of the World series (Methuen)

Arts & Crafts of South America
Lucy Davies and Mo Fini (Tumi)

Instruments Around the World
Andy Jackson (Longman)

Jamaican Music; Indian Music; The Steel Band
Michael Burett
(Oxford University Press)

Making Musical Instruments
Margaret McLean (Macmillan)

Mango & Spice: 44 Caribbean Songs
The Singing Sack: 28 Songs from Around the World
(A & C Black)

Music of the World
Alan Blackwood (Facts on File)

Musical Instruments
(*Sticky Fingers* series)
Ting Morris (Watts Books)

Musical Instruments of the World
Diagram Group (Facts on File)

Our Steel Band
Rachel Warner (Hamish Hamilton)

Scrape, Rattle and Blow
Chris Deshpande (A & C Black)

Vibrations
David Sawyer
(Cambridge University Press)

The Watts Book of Music
Keith Spence (Watts Books)

World Crafts
Jacqueline Herald (Oxfam)

Australia

Some helpful addresses

Hobby Co
197 Pitt Street
Sydney NSW 2000

Edgeworth Craft Supplies
63 Edgeworth David Avenue
Waitara NSW 2077

Elsa's Folk Art Studio & Supplies
12 Myrtle Street
Normanhurst NSW 2076

Powerhouse Museum
Harris Street
Ultimo NSW 2007

Glossary

aerophone A musical instrument that works by vibrating air against a sharp edge.

amplify To make louder.

bridge A piece of wood or other material over which strings are stretched.

calabash The hard shell of a gourd or other tropical fruit that is used as a container.

ceramic Made of pottery.

chamois leather Soft leather from a sheep, goat or deer.

chordophone A musical instrument that works by vibrating strings.

conical Cone-shaped.

Coptic Belonging to the Copts, a group of Christians originally from Egypt.

cylindrical In the shape of a cylinder or tube.

flat A musical term that means below the normal pitch of a note.

***gamelan* orchestra** A group of Indonesian musicians who play at religious ceremonies, dances and puppet plays.

hide Skin of an animal.

ideophone A musical instrument that is designed to use the natural sounds of different materials.

inlaid work A way of decorating a wooden surface by fitting different coloured woods into it.

linguaphone A musical instrument that works by vibrating a 'tongue' of metal or other material.

membranophone A musical instrument that works by vibrating a skin, or membrane.

modification A change that makes something work better.

morris dancer Traditional English folk dancer.

Pan The Greek god of woods and pastures.

pitch The quality of a musical note. Pitch is measured by the rate of vibrations.

resonator A box or container that makes a note sound louder.

sharp A musical term that means higher than the normal pitch of a note.

uncured Describes an animal skin before it has been treated to make it supple.

vessel A container such as a pot or jar.

vibrate To move backwards and forwards very quickly.

Index

Additional photographs:

page 12 (bottom), Christine Osborne Pictures; page 14 (top), page 22 (right), page 24 (right), Robert Harding Picture Library.